Let's EXPLORE

baby einstein.

Animals

Photo Credits:
Dog Lon E. Lauber © Oxford Scientific Film • *Tiger* © Alan & Sandy Carey • *Cat* © 2001 Martial
Colomb • *Elephant* © Jeremy Woodhouse • *Duck* Alvis Upitis © Image Bank • *Sea Turtle* David
B. Fleetham © Oxford Scientific Film • *Otter* © Ian Cartwright • *Frog* Joseph Devenney © Image
Bank • *Monkey* Michael Sewell © Oxford Scientific Film • *Mouse* Ian West © Oxford Scientific
Film • *Giraffe* © Jeremy Woodhouse • *Rabbit* Michael Powles © Oxford Scientific Film • *Bear*
Daniel J. Cox © Oxford Scientific Film • *Cow* Russel © Oxford Scientific Film • *Lion* © Jeremy
Woodhouse • *Squirrel* Micael Melford © Image Bank

Visit www.hyperionbooksforchildren.com and www.babyeinstein.com

Great Minds Start Little.™

This is a golden retriever.

Dog facts

- Dogs give people kisses with their wet tongues.

- Dogs are very loyal animals and are sometimes called 'man's best friend.'

- Dogs were the first animals to live with people as pets.

- Some dogs help people who are blind or disabled, and some dogs help police officers find people who are missing.

This is a Bengal tiger.

Tiger facts

- Most tigers are orange and white with dark stripes. A few tigers are all white with dark stripes.

- The tiger's front paws are almost twice as big as its back paws.

- Tigers hunt animals such as wild pigs, cattle and deer.

- The tiger is the largest cat in the world; an adult male can weigh up to 500 pounds (227kg).

- Each tiger has its own pattern of stripes. Like human fingerprints, no two stripes are the same.

Cat facts

- Cats make a lot of sounds. They meow, purr, hiss, growl and screech.

- A cat cleans its fur by licking itself with its rough tongue.

- Cats don't like to get wet!

- Cats have special eyes that can see six times better than ours.

- Many people keep cats as pets. Tigers, lions, leopards and panthers are some of the cat's wild relatives.

This is an African elephant.

Elephant facts

- An elephant uses its trunk like a hand to pick up food and wash itself with water.

- A baby elephant often uses its trunk to hold on to its mother's tail.

- Elephants are herbivores; they eat things like hay, grass and other plants.

- Elephants spend most of their lives traveling across the savannah.

This duck is a mallard.

Duck facts

- Ducks always live near the water.

- A mother duck keeps her ducklings together to protect them.

- During the winter, many ducks fly long distances to get to warmer places where the water won't freeze.

- A duck has webbed feet that act like paddles when it swims.

- A baby duck is called a duckling.

This is a green sea turtle.

Sea turtle facts

- The feet and legs of sea turtles are shaped like flippers. This makes them strong swimmers.

- Unlike other turtles, sea turtles can't pull their heads and legs into their shells.

- Sea turtles eat sea grass and other plants in the ocean, jellyfish, squids and sea urchins.

- Mother sea turtles come ashore to lay eggs. They dig their nests in sandy beaches, then bury the eggs in the sand.

Otter facts

- Otters often dive for their food. They eat things like fish, crabs, clams and frogs.

- Sea otters float on their backs while they eat, using their belly as a table.

- Most otters have webbed feet. This makes them strong swimmers.

- The otter's thick fur is waterproof and keeps it warm in cold water.

- Otters live near rivers, lakes and streams. Sea otters live in the ocean, but they are never far from shore.

This is a gray tree frog.

Frog facts

- Some frogs are very colorful, though most are green or brown.

- Many frogs have long, strong, back legs which they use to jump and swim.

- Frogs eat insects, earthworms and spiders. They capture food with their long, sticky tongues.

- Many frogs begin their life in water as a tadpole. Tadpoles have long tails and look like small fish.

These are Patas monkeys.

Monkey facts

- Many monkeys live in the jungle. Jungle monkeys spend most of their time in the trees.

- Most monkeys have strong tails. Some use their tails to grab tree branches.

- Newborn monkeys hold on to their mother's belly. When they get older, they ride on their mother's back.

- Monkeys often live in large groups. One adult male is usually the leader of the group.

This is a yellow-necked mouse.

Mouse facts

- Mice have round ears, a thin tail and soft fur. They can be brown, grey, white or spotted.

- Mice like to eat many different things such as seeds, berries, insects, nuts and plants.

- A baby mouse is born without fur and has pink skin.

- Mice live in fields, forests, mountains and deserts. Some mice live in people's homes!

- A mouse uses its sharp front teeth to chew on things. These teeth never stop growing.

This is an African giraffe.

Giraffe facts

- The giraffe is the tallest animal in the world.

- When baby giraffes are born they are already taller than many grown-up people.

- The giraffe's long neck allows it to eat leaves from the tops of trees. It has a long tongue that can grab leaves and branches.

- The giraffe's spots make it almost invisible in a tree's shadow. This is called camouflage.

Rabbit Facts

- A rabbit has long ears and a short, fluffy tail.

- Rabbits hop using their long hind legs.

- A rabbit eats grass and plants. Some rabbits sneak vegetables from people's gardens!

- Rabbits live in grasslands, deserts, forests and swamps. They usually make their homes in holes or burrows.

This is a grizzly bear.

Bear facts

- There are many different kinds of bears. Some are black and brown. There are even white bears.

- Most bears eat both plants and meat. They like fruit, berries, nuts, fish and honey.

- Bears are excellent at catching fish. They use their big paws and claws to catch fish in rivers and streams.

- Many bears sleep through most of the winter. This is called hibernation.

This is a Fresian cow.

Cow facts

- Cows are important farm animals. Some people get milk from cows.

- A cow may be black, white or brown. Cows have long tails, and some cows have horns.

- A female cow's udder hangs below its body. The udder holds the cow's milk.

- Cows eat grass on prairies and plains. This is called grazing.

- Many cows together are called a herd.

This is a Kalahari lion.

Lion facts

- A male lion's roar is so loud it can be heard up to five miles away!

- Male lions have big manes of hair that cover their necks. Females do not.

- Female lions and their children live in family groups called prides.

- Most lions live in the African grasslands, which are called the savannah.

This is a gray squirrel.

Squirrel facts

- Squirrels eat nuts, seeds and fruits. A squirrel will often bury extra food to eat later.

- Squirrels live in woods, parks and yards. They build their nests in tree branches, tree trunks or burrows.

- The squirrel's bushy tail helps it to balance on tree branches.